THE LAUGHTER
OF MOTHERS

Paul Durcan

The Laughter
of Mothers

Harvill *Secker*
LONDON

Published by Harvill Secker 2007

2 4 6 8 10 9 7 5 3 1

First published in Great Britain in 2007 by
HARVILL SECKER
Random House, 20 Vauxhall Bridge Road
London SW1V 2SA

www.rbooks.co.uk

Addresses for companies within The Random House Group Limited
can be found at: www.randomhouse.co.uk/offices.htm

The Random House Group Limited Reg. No. 954009

A CIP catalogue record for this book is available from
the British Library

ISBN 9781846550232

The Random House Group Limited makes every effort to ensure that
the papers used in its books are made from trees that have been legally
sourced from well-managed and credibly certified forests. Our paper
procurement policy can be found at:
www.randomhouse.co.uk/paper.htm

Typeset in Bembo by Palimpsest Book Production Limited,
Grangemouth, Stirlingshire

Printed and bound in Germany by
GGP Media GmbH, Pößneck

to the memory of
Sheila MacBride Durcan
of Westport, County Mayo
1915–2004

Acknowledgements

'A Single Red Rose for the Last Boy King' appeared in *Jack B. Yeats* (Waddington Galleries / Theo Waddington, London, 2005). 'Kneeling at the Last Wave' was published in *Northabout* by Jarlath Cunnane (Cork, 2006).

Contents

The Laughter of Mothers

Mrs Barrington-Stuart's Version of What Happened

Mr Barrington-Stuart and I were driving west from Dublin
To spend our annual holiday in Renvyle.
We stopped at Lough Owel to picnic
As we always stop at Lough Owel to picnic.
For fifty-five years we have always stopped at Lough Owel.
We spread out our Foxford rug at the top of the bank
In the same place we have always spread out our Foxford rug.
There we were, sitting erect on our Foxford rug,
Having our picnic lunch in silence,
Enjoying Lough Owel and the islands,
Our cucumber sandwiches and our flask of tea,
When Mr Barrington-Stuart turned over on his side
Like he does in bed in the middle of the night
And, before I could take another bite of my sandwich,
He had begun rolling down the bank.
He rolled all the way down the bank into the lake
And, before I could stand up, he had passed away.
You can imagine how surprised I was.
Nobody would believe me in Renvyle.

A Gynaecologist in Dubai
Fishing at Evening

Taking stock of my life, I am somewhat surprised
By what I have achieved in what is a short time
Sub specie aeternitatis.
By the age of forty-five I was a millionaire
Twice over and now at sixty-five
Here I am, an ordinary Dublin man,
With my own five-bedroom apartment in Dubai
As a bolt-hole from my Edwardian mansion in Dublin.
It's pleasant to get away from the rain and the cold
For a couple of weeks as well as from the job –
I do get somewhat bored, not to say somewhat impatient
With all these women discovering childbirth
As if nobody before them in history
Had ever given birth to an infant.
Fishing at evening in the Sheikh Muhammad Abdullah lake
(Built incidentally by Byrne Brothers of Dublin),
Fondling my rod, I come to thinking
That the secret of a successful life such as mine
Resides in my selection of hooks over a lifetime:
Obstetrics, golf, Thai wife, house.
I caught all the right fish.
I am somewhat proud of being Irish
At the commencement of the twenty-first century.

The Story of Ireland

The single most crucial factor in twentieth-century Irish
    history was golf.

Had it not been for golf, the country would have relapsed
    into barbarism.

When the going got bad, men put their heads down and
    played golf.

In a crisis a man put on his golf gloves.

On Sunday mornings good men went to the golf course
    instead of to church.

The bank manager arranged to meet the bank robber on the
    golf course.

When a marriage looked like going on the rocks

A husband and wife started playing golf in their home.

While the husband did putting practice in the bathroom

The wife practised her swing in the drawing room.

In bed the wife would say to her husband:

'Imagine you're playing an approach shot with a number
    seven iron.'

Later she'd add:

'Imagine you're putting for the match.'

And finally:

'I'll pretend I didn't see you miss your putt.'

Or simply:

'I'll give you your putt.'

Golf brought back civilisation to Ireland in the twentieth century

So that in the twenty-first century even Sinn Féin started
   playing golf
As well as going into buying and selling
Golf courses in Kazakhstan and Siberia, and most recently
   China.
It is reported by the Belfast News Agency WEDGE
That 27 per cent of Chinese golf courses are owned by Sinn
   Féin.
Sinn Féin's showpiece
Is the Mao Golf and Country Club in Shanghai,
Which worldwide is second only
To the Roman Catholic Church's operation
On the West Coast of Ireland –
The Pope John Paul II Golf and Country Club in Galway
   Bay
On the site of what used be the city of Galway
And for the building and development of which the city was
   demolished
In 2005 and, courtesy of Allied Irish Banks,
Transferred to Pittsville, Pennsylvania.
The *craic* is said to be gosh-darned okay in Pittsville.

Death on Strand Road

Passers-by stop to try and help the dying man
As he lies flat on his back in the yellow box
Of the On the Run filling station on Strand Road,
A *few* passers-by but not *all* passers-by.
Some do not notice, some are in too much of a hurry
To pay for their petrol or to purchase their newspapers,
Their take-away coffee, their sausage rolls,
To stop to help a man in his death-throes
At half-eleven in the morning on a Thursday in November,
His face changing colour by the second
From grey to red to purple to black
Like a lost sheepdog on its back having nightmares.
He is stretched out beside his silver Ford Focus 5-door
    Estate
In which ninety seconds ago he had been cruising along
Strand Road, admiring the seascape
When his heart blew up. He pulled in
To the filling station, got out, fell down
At the door signed FIRE EXIT! KEEP CLEAR.
The few passers-by who do have time to stop
Do everything they can to resuscitate the dying man:
Three American policemen on holiday in Ireland
Jumping out of a hired Toyota Space Wagon,
Giving him the kiss of life, pounding his chest;
Trying to keep him alive, if he is still alive,

Until the ambulance and fire brigade swoop up,
Scoop him up, rush him away
Down along Strand Road to St Vincent's Hospital,
The tide out, a man in red on the black sands
With a bucket and spade, digging for worms.
The polite young manager of On the Run
In his smart brown-and-yellow uniform
Stands with a clipboard taking names of witnesses,
A young mother in boots pushing a baby buggy trots off
With a muffin in a paper bag bearing the logo
On the Run – A Fresh Call Every Time.
The silver Ford Focus 5-door Estate
Stands out-of-focus, abandoned, forlorn, empty,
A blue Ordnance Survey Dublin Street Atlas lying open on
    the front passenger seat
Like another lost sheepdog, pleading, beseeching, inquiring
'Where is Tritonville Road?' or
'Am I an actor in a play?' or
'Do you believe in reincarnation?'
Before being obscured from view, blacked out
By a convoy of artics crashing past to the East Link Toll
    Bridge.
On a trolley in A&E in St Vincent's Hospital
Lies a man's lifeless corpse which but eleven minutes ago
Was a living body on four wheels cruising along Strand
    Road,
Much of a mild winter's day ahead of him,
Six weeks to Christmas. The polite young manager
Of On the Run blurts out: 'The Lord have mercy on his
    soul.'

In the Shopping Spree on the Last Sunday before Christmas

Spotting, whilst I reversed into a tight parking space,
A traveller woman in a doorway assessing me,
I realised she was about to pounce on me.
Dutifully, as it seemed, she was about to pounce on
    me,
Stocky tanned lady with jet-black hair in a ponytail.
As I sidled away from my car, double-locking it with
    the remote,
She stepped out in front of me barring the way
And before I could say anything, she declaimed
In the voice of an old-world actor-manager playing the
    female lead:
'Don't worry, sir, I'm not going to beg from you,
I only want to tell you a story,
Because I can see you have a face on you.
None of these people will even look at me!'
She declaimed, gesticulating at the passers-by.
'I only want to tell you, sir,
That I am a human being
And that my daughter here also beside me
Is a human being,
A poor, little thrawneen of a god-forsaken human
    being.
They don't consider us as human beings

But we are human beings, sir. I need seventy euro
To get the boat to England. My husband
Is after beating me up, no word of a lie.'
Knowing I had a ten-euro note in my breast pocket
I fished it out and put it in her hand.
She shut her eyes and pursed her lips
And she shouted 'The Lord have mercy on you, sir!
But how am I to get to England?
How am I to cross over the bitter sea?'
Whereupon I fished out another ten-euro note
And handed it to her. Her outrage
And grief intensified as she continued shouting:
'I have eleven stitches in the back of my head
On account of my husband, he broke a bottle across it,
And my daughter has four stitches in the back of *her*
    head.
I wish to holy God I had never got married!
Sir, I know you have a fifty-euro note in your pocket,
If you give it to me, I'll do overtime praying for you.'
How did she know I had a fifty-euro note
In my pocket? Is she a psychic?
I handed it to her, stammering
'W-what is your name and w-where are you from?'
She answered me proudly: 'I'm Mamie Thornton and
    I'm from Galway
And my daughter is Tina
And she has eaten nothing for near on three weeks
And I'll say a prayer for you to the holy mother of
    God if
You give me that other fifty-euro note in your pocket.'

I shouted back at her, 'But Mamie, Mamie –
I don't have another fifty-euro note!'
'But I have to get the boat to England!' she shouted.
I began to hurry away, but she hurried with me:
'I can see, sir, you have time for people.
Most people have no time for people.
I know that because I'm from Galway.
Now give me two hundred euro and I will pray
For a month to Our Lady of Fatima for you.'
'Please Mamie,' I begged her, 'please Mamie –
I don't have two hundred euro to give you!'
'Oh but you do, sir,' she whispered. 'Oh but you do, sir.'
Bestowing on me a wounded, reserved look of
    contemptuous compassion,
She turned her back on me and waddled off
And her teenage daughter clinging to her arm started
    to laugh
And to stare at me as if I was some new class of a
    settled madman
She had never set eyes on before.
In the winter sunlight under blue skies
In the shopping spree on the last Sunday before
    Christmas
I stood rooted to the footpath looking after them, lost
    in admiration.

Christmas Week

Sitting on the rocks on midwinter's day
With my flask of coffee
I am drawing a ship at anchor on the skyline
When a voice up above me barks
From the pathway of the promenade
'What are you doing?'
I look around and behold above me
The shoulders of a successful career woman.
Her mouth-corners are nooses of affluence,
Her eyes slot machines in the jigs.

She is enjoying looking down at me
And she repeats: 'What are you doing
Down there on the rocks in the middle of winter?'
I smile a seasonal smile
But I do not answer her.
She walks off
With that superior waddle of hers,
Her loins billowing in sensible slacks
And I retrieve the serenity of drawing
A ship at anchor on the skyline
And the other lines of Dublin Bay.

Lines are what I like:
Lines of water, lines of sand-plain,
Lines of seaweed, lines of geese,
Lines of chimneys, lines of spires,
Lines of cranes, lines of airplanes.
I draw what I like, I like what I draw.
I am not an artist, but I get pleasure
Drawing lines I like
On the rocks in the middle of winter.
On a winter's day on the empty shore
I confide in lines of water and sky,
Keeping away from the cold souls of people.

Lecarrow Harbour

That the smooth blue-and-white lake
Flew into a tantrum;
That we, a small family
In a hired launch, an Emerald Star
Four-berther, a young father and mother
With two small girls, all of a sudden
Were battling for our lives on a summer's day:
These are the headlines that rear tears in my eyes
As this afternoon twenty-one years later
I revisit the harbour that saved our lives;
The name of which none of us could ever forget
In spite of all the lives we would live
And all the roads that would scatter us:
Lecarrow Harbour.

Caught out in the middle of Lough Ree
In a whiplash maelstrom of wind and rain
With nothing between ourselves and the rocks
But a loose fixed compass and a torn wet map
On which we could see, or thought
We could see, north north-west, an inlet
Named Blackbrink Bay
Into which a canal had been cut
For a mile and a half inland
To Lecarrow Harbour.

Our two children in lifejackets crouched in the cabin
As their mother took the wheel
And their father stood at her side
Grappling to relate compass to map,
Trying to chart a course –
Trying to call it out and be heard –
Between St John's Bay and the Black Islands.
They could see nothing but the black waves
Rearing white heads over the bow;
They could hear only the winds
Gusting to gales
And their two parents shouting
And their own voices yelling
And they both felt too petrified to feel afraid.

God clicked the camera of Life and Death
And through its aperture we wriggled
Into Blackbrink Bay; the gale
In the reeds a lullaby to our escape
From the gale on the lake tearing up
The scrolls of the waters.
Along the slim canal we inched
For a mile and a half, each of us
Quivering in our knowledge of death.
Under slow, hilly fields of sheep
We chugged into the world's end,
A stone-clad pen with capstans
And wide steps: Lecarrow Harbour.

Whatever number of days we stayed
In Lecarrow Harbour, to us
It was a lifetime – a lifetime
Of playing hide-and-go seek in the young limes,
A lifetime of sanctuary,
A lifetime of sitting still on the jetty wall
Watching two small girls, curly sisters
Squawking as they paddled around
In the jollyboat among ducks and drakes
Whilst up in the grass in the birch trees
Shelves of chicks sat in their half-dozens.

This afternoon in Lecarrow Harbour
A lone woman sailor in a rickety skiff
Is hanging out tea towels to dry
From a multi-branched clothes hanger
Swaying from a birch-branch.
Ducks and drakes patrol the waters,
Their multitudinous young
In flocks up on the banks.
My elder daughter is expecting next month,
Her younger sister the month after,
Their mother secure in her Cork city nest
With her caretaker man.
In the silence I say prayers
Of thanksgiving and praise
For my daughters and their husbands
And the sane woman of Cork

Before driving off into yet another storm
Lurching in from the northwest,
Beating up black clouds
Low on the hills of Roscommon.

Fathers and Daughters

. . . but what she does not know as she hangs out the
 washing
On a line strung between two ash trees in a field
In the middle of a small island on the edge of Europe
And a peg slips off the line and she lets drop
A white shirt in the grass, her father in a suburb
Of a small town in Central Europe is being captured
 on CCTV
In the act of stumbling on the kerb of an automobile-
 abounding street
And losing his footing, both feet going from under
 him,
He who is a fifty-nine-year-old pedestrian,
And falling on his face head-first full-length on the
 street
Under automobiles whose braking tyres swerve around
 him.
She chides the dropped shirt but smiles to herself as her
 eyes
Feast on the new green grass under her feet and the
 dock leaves and buttercups
And the breeze in her face and the sun piercing the
 treetops;
He is picking himself up off the street, his right knee
 bleeding,

His shoulder not answering to him, his ankle stinging,
As he limps away towards the pizzeria where he must
    eat alone
For the ninth night in a row, trying to pretend that
    nothing has happened.
He sits hunched in the pizzeria, hunched over a pizza,
Trying not to feel sorry for himself, trying
To remember a psalm, any psalm, Psalm 133:
'It is like the dew of Hermon which falls on the
    heights of Zion.'
He repeats to himself the refrain of her text message:
'Hope you're having a great time in Poland.'
Skipping away from the clothes line, she cries out: 'Ye
    Gods! Shit!'

Achill Island Girl

I was born in Murphysboro, Illinois, in 1990,
My parents' eldest daughter.
They christened me Saoirse,
Which is the Irish word for Liberty.
It's the best thing they did,
Christening me Saoirse.
There are lots of things I like doing and being,
But best of all is to hear a voice
Calling me by the name my parents christened me,
Someone, anyone, calling out my name across the
   bridge
Or repeating my name into a mobile,
Saoirse, Saoirse.
My name is a war cry for peace.
But when at band practice in the community hall
The pipe major starts chanting my name high above
   the pipes
My eyes fill with cliffs
And the one hundred-and-sixteen freckles on my
   cheeks begin to swim
Off the edge of my face
And I want to run to my mother and throw my arms
   around her neck,
My father sitting at the head of the table reading from
   a history book to her.

Mr and Mrs Henry

5 a.m. Tuesday May 29, 2001:
I am hearing voices under my dormer window
In the house at the foot of the mountain.

Realising that I am not dreaming,
I stumble out of bed and look down:
I see Mrs Henry in her pink dressing gown

Wrestling with a lamb, grappling to
Untangle it from the wire fence;
The lamb is mute, prone, vertical

Like a carcass hanging from a meat-hook.
'Come and give me a hand, Don.'
'Wait till the morning, Thelma.'

Don's full tide of Dublin working-class vowels
Swirls in and around and out
The sand-castles of Thelma's Dublin middle-class
    consonants.

Don and Thelma are Dubliners on Achill Island
Who have sold up their home in Dublin.
Although they have at least two great grandchildren

They are as youthful a married couple
As you could hope to meet.
Gleefully bickering; together forever.

'The lamb will die, Don,' Thelma scolds him.
Don lopes out with a pair of pliers.
Three snips and the lamb skips free.

Mr and Mrs Henry would shame you,
Know-alls of the airwaves and the broadsheets.
While I sigh my way back into my single bed

They gambol across the gravel,
Bouncing back into their bedroom.
Spicy old Dubs of the mountain.

A View of the Bridge

I was standing at the window of my shoe shop at
    eleven o'clock in the morning
Admiring the baskets of flowers on the lamp-posts that
    we'd hung up the previous week
And wondering if I'd bother buying a national
    newspaper across the river in McGreevy's –
What's the point in buying a national newspaper?
    Maybe I should be thinking
About buying a copy of the *International Herald Tribune*
    if it's in –
When who do I see coming over the bridge, the
    three-arched bridge in the centre of our town,
But Seamus Heaney and John McGahern, our two
    world-famous authors, strolling slowly,
Strolling *very* slowly, fresh as daisies, arm in arm at
    eleven o'clock in the morning.
Fresh as daisies, yet men of an older vintage than me.
I couldn't believe it. It was about four years ago. I ran
    back into the shop
And fetched out the great ledger that we've had for a
    hundred-and-two years and a fountain pen
And I went to rush out the door only for my guardian
    angel to grab me by the scruff of the neck.
'Woa boy, woa, boy, woa, woa!' my guardian angel
    neighed into my ear

As I gawked out the door at the two world-famous
    authors as they stood
At the end of the bridge on my side of the river
    glancing over at my shoe shop –
Or seeming to, for they were totally engrossed in their
    conversation.
They looked like two sheep farmers after coming out
    of Sunday Mass,
In their Sunday half-best, black slacks, black slip-ons,
    tweed jackets, open-neck white shirts,
Not so much striking a bargain between themselves as
    discussing
A grander bargain having been struck somewhere else
    that they had witnessed.
For the love of God, I muttered to myself, it's not
    every day or every week
Or every year or every hundred years that you'd see
    two world-famous authors
Walking the streets of a small town in the west of
    Ireland and yet –
What right have I to interrupt their morning, their
    morning stroll,
Their conversation, their sacred conversation? 'Holy God,'
I roared at myself, 'but you have no right to do such a
    thing!'
I put down the great ledger of 1903 on the counter
And folded my arms and crossed my legs and
    immediately
I felt an indescribable surge of surprise and good
    fortune and common sense

As I watched them turn around under a high basket of
fresh flowers and walk off down along the river into
the trees.
In our small town we may be behind the times in lots
of ways, but we're no huxters like some I won't
name in big cities not far away, isn't life gas?

Tesco's

My husband quit work years ago
Before we split up.
Quite a busy little consultant
He was, quite in demand.
That was one of the reasons
I left him – when he decided
To stop working and he
Hung around all day,
Getting on my janglies.
Anyway I met this other male,
This other maelstrom.
I met him in Alicante.
He's an entrepreneur in Cork and he's got
Dough and he's not
The ugliest male in town
And, you know, well,
He's much older than me
But he's all right.
He drives a 60 K Land Rover
And I said to myself: this is it,
This is the product I'm looking for,
This is the ukelele I'll spend
The rest of my lonesome with, only
After six months what do I find out
But that he's an alcoholic.

It took me all of six months
To notice that he was an alcoholic.
I'm slow on the uptake.
No, it wasn't the drunk driving
That put me off him
So much as his thing at breakfast
Of putting whisky in his cup of tea.
That really stuck in my craw!
Drink-driving a 60 K Land Rover
You don't really mind having an accident,
Because you know it won't be you
That will be killed or maimed or whatever.
Putting whisky in his cup of tea,
The cheek of him! I haven't seen him
In yonks and I would not be
At all gobsmacked to hear
That he had kicked the bucket.
To get over him – and I really
Did vaguely like him –
Myself and Bim, my daughter,
Decided to take a break in Chile.
Bim's doing Business Studies in DCU.
Coolest holiday I ever had.
We bought an old banger for nothing
From an old dude in Buenos Aires –
Is Buenos Aires in Chile?
No, it's not – the other place,
I mean, what do you call it? –
Valaparadiso!
We drove down to Patagonia

And all the way to Terra del Foco.
We adored Terra del Foco.
Oh God! Have you done your shopping?
Tesco's is the end, isn't it?

Women's Fashions Return to Roots

Last year it was the bare belly-button look
But this year the midriff has been all closed up
And instead it's the bare-bottom look –
Two holes cut in the seat of the jeans –
More eyelets than holes.
It's called 'The Monkey Look' and it's become an
    epidemic.

At Mass this morning the new look was on parade.
I had no choice but to study it at close quarters.
In the pew in front of me three teenage sisters
Stood each with two holes in the seat of their jeans
Revealing small circular areas of off-white flesh:
'The Monkey Look' on the 23rd Sunday in Ordinary
    Time.

Each of the three teenage sisters draped an infant over
    her shoulder
So that, confronted with bare bottoms and bawling
    infants,
It was not difficult to imagine oneself
Back in the mountain forests of the Congo
Among clusters of primates with their offspring.
'Returning to your roots' is what it is called.

Coincidentally the reading was Paul, Romans 13: 8–10,
In which that gregarious evangelist states that
'Love is what it's all about.'
Contemplating reluctantly the bare bottoms and the
bawling infants
I thought many heretical thoughts, but chiefly:
Love is something to be avoided at all costs.

Surgery Story

You know my friend Louis Rabbitte, don't you?
I thought you did. Anyway,
I was best man at his wedding.
His wife (*makes a drinking gesture with elbow and wrist*
Indicating a glass being gulped back) . . .
Anyway, their son Dylan
Is an independent young fellow.
He has a Dublin accent, the full monty.
Shaven head. Ear-ring in the nostril.
He drives an HGV Dublin–Belfast every day.
He telephoned me one day here in the surgery.
I'd a patient prostrate in the chair.
My secretary said: 'There is a Dylan
On the line, he says he knows you.'
It's Dylan Rabbitte – Louis Rabbitte's boy.
He says to me in the Dublin accent:
'All my dad's friends are well-off like you,
So I thought I'd rob each of you of just one item,
But so as not to break any windows or doors
Or hurt anyone's feelings
I decided to ask each of you
To leave me out just one piece of silverware
On the patio deck, early on Sunday morning.
Will you do that for me?
Jayzus, you're a fuggen Christian.'

Isn't he an enterprising young fellow?
His mother *(repeats drinking gesture with elbow and wrist Indicating a glass being gulped back)* . . .

A Toad in October
Swimming at Dawn

Palpitating on the pond's rim, I am stilled
To see a large male toad in the water floundering
Under the weight of what appears
To be a growth on his back,
An ugly-looking excrescence.

Close-up it is not a malignant growth
But another toad – the female –
A third of his size and riding on his back
With her two webbed feet fastened
Around his armpits
And with her hind legs she goads him
When he looks like slacking.

They could not be more different from one another –
Almost as incongruous as their human counterparts –
Her short squat green-black torso up above
His pink-brown leopard-skin long white legs,
His pink-brown leopard-skin long white arms,
His Churchillian eyes glaring out of Neanderthal sockets.

Continually he looks like sinking under her weight,
But I stifle my fellow-feelings of compassion and empathy

When I take cognisance of his prehensile webbed feet:
With such dinosaur tentacles the male toad of the species
Can look after himself (and herself)

I turn away and retrace my pre-breakfast morning steps
Across the soaking clover.
'Does God exist?' is the wrong question.
'Is it a natural thing to sing a psalm of praise?'
Is the proper question:
And the answer, I can see, cannot be but yes.

Women Are the Shape of Things to Come

In theology, not in sexuality, dwells the magnetism of
    women:
A woman by definition is a walking resurrection.

'The World of William Orpen'

I am a woman robed in black
For whom the years are my tears,
Playing the harp for my living.

For the opening of 'The World of William Orpen'
The National Gallery installed me
At the top of the staircase of the millennium wing.

For the art lovers of Dublin
I plucked Edwardian airs
And Carolan and Moore and Harty.

I was staring in stupefaction
At the happy throng when through my strings
I glimpsed a small girl

In a blue denim coat returning my stare,
Only her stare was sparkling with wet smiles
Like the sea in the sun

As she stared at my fingers wheeling,
Entranced under the harp's prow,
All her life before her.

Innocence is the prospect of innocence,
The cliff, the shore, the ocean,
That gauntlet beyond the horizon

In whose spotlight now I crouch,
Going through the agony of my mimicry,
Numb to everything except a small girl's spasm.

A Single Red Rose for the
Last Boy King

In the souk of my demise,
The walled canals of Dublin,
In my gold chemise
I lay me down unknown:
Jack B. Yeats, boy alone.

On Being Required to Remove
My Trouser Belt at
Dublin Airport Security

Holding up my trousers with my hands – what
Would Saddam have to say, indignant
In the dock in Baghdad at not having a pen? –
  although
I feel and look ridiculous and ludicrous, at least
I will pass through the detector without the alarm
  going off, but –
Bingo! – the light on top of the detector emits a cry
And I freeze in the frame, what can it be, I
Look down between my legs.
Is it my libido? My portable libido?
My portable libido making a last stand?
Does Saddam have a portable libido?
No, I would not like to see Saddam's portable libido.
Put away your portable libido, Saddam,
Put away your prickly pop-up
And you too, Tony, and you, George, Silvio, Vladimir,
Conformists the lot of you,
All wearing the same uniform,
The identical pinstripe tight mini-skirt,
Regulation four inches above the knee.
Stop it this minute!

Stop looking between your legs!
The security man gropes me and
I hold tightly on to my trousers: Oh
God no, this is not the way I wanted to exit,
Holding up my trousers with my hands, no,
I will not! I let go.
I let my trousers drop to the floor, let
Them think I am an eccentric, everybody
Ought to be an eccentric. I step
Out of my green cords, depositing them
Under the detector, a puddle of green blood.
I am pleased with myself, I doubt
If Saddam would have had the aplomb to do that
Nor Tony nor George nor Vladimir nor Silvio.
I tip-toe up and down the duty free
Holding my trousers on my arm
Until another security man, unashamed
Of his native courtesy and his broad Dublin accent,
Encourages me to put them back on.
'Would you be a good man now and put your trousers
    back on?'
I could imagine him saying the same to Saddam:
'Would you be a good man now Saddam and put your
    trousers back on?'
Or to Tony or George or Vladimir or Silvio.
It's a fine thing to be courteous to a naked man, even
If he's a war-leader with a prickly pop-up.

29 November 2005

On My Sixty-First Birthday

Late in the afternoon
The sun is going down,
It is getting colder and colder
Darkness is spreading.

In my striped pyjamas
I stand at the window
Shouting into the street below
'Help! Help!'

Nobody takes any notice,
All seems hopeless,
But then a surprise occurs:
The street lights come on.

The Waterford Relays

to Mark Quinn

Running the relay at twelve
Is not half so good an idea
As running the relay at sixty-two.
It's not only that at sixty-two
I drop the baton,
Which is normal,
But that I arrive at the handover without the baton,
Having forgotten to start with the baton in the first place,
Which is even more normal.
Nobody knows who I am
On whom even the clouds shine.

On the Dublin–Sligo
Commuter Train

On the Dublin-Sligo commuter train
Faced with a young man in the seat opposite me
Who picked his nose all the way from Dublin to Sligo
And deposited the upshot on his blue jeans,
Rubbing the stuff hard in,
And, on top of that, while he excavated each nostril,
Dredging its mucous,
He not only read the *Irish Independent*
From front page to back page
But he read it, rattling its pages,
Tearing at them, flapping them,
As if there was no one else in the coach.
What was I to do to stay sane?
I took out a memo book and biro
And I scrawled the most defamatory things I could think of,
Hoping the stingrays of my defamations
Would render or at least immobilise him,
In the words of Milton,
'Nose-picking little moron.'
Dumbly I roared at the gods
To curse the parents that raised him,
His slit-eyed, freckled, red-headed breed
And all their seed

And I stood up with a jolt
And put my two hands on the ledge
Of the overhead rack
And, invoking all the deer on the mountain,
I shook my head
But he took not the blindest bit of notice
And I had to slink back down into my seat
And seethe all the way across Ireland into Sligo.

At the Grave of My Aunt Sara Mary

At the grave of my aunt Sara Mary the family
Have inserted a cuckoo clock in the headstone
Under the names of my grandfather and grandmother.
There was no space on the headstone for Sara Mary's
    name,
So her name was incised on the rear of the headstone
Under the statue of the Virgin Mary, the hem
Of the Virgin's cloak grazing Sara Mary's name.
I falter in front of her grave attempting to pray to her
In spite of her name being on the rear of the headstone
And not realising that the clock is active.
The clock chimes and from behind shut, louvred doors
Out hops a cuckoo – only it is not a cuckoo,
It is a tiny wooden painted statuette of my spinster aunt
Flapping her blue woolly arms and bowing up and down,
Calling out her favourite vocable: ''Ospital! 'Ospital!',
('Life is an 'ospital,' she used cry to us children
In her spasm-smiling voice),
Her benignant bosom kicking up under a blue cardigan,
Her red face beaming, her waist-length grey hair
Piled high on her head in a nest,
Just as in life, teeming with anticipation,
Throbbing with expectation, tears of laughter
Brimming her eyes, she used welcome us children home
To the home of our ancestors.

After five chimes —
It is five in the afternoon on the 22nd of June —
''Ospital! 'Ospital! 'Ospital! 'Ospital! 'Ospital!' —
She hops back in and the doors slam shut.
I climb the graveyard to the round tower
And the roofless church with the medieval carving
Over the lintel of a boy Christ with spiked hair,
Splayed hands, splayed knees,
A hand-towel for a loincloth, jiving the Crucifixion
On midsummer's night at sunrise.

My aunt's life was also a crucifixion,
Which she danced with an abandon no one else
In the family could equal. They all motored off
To the cities and the towns to lead professional lives
Of privilege and luxury, property and holiday,
While she stayed at home to run the public house
With oil lamps and water from the well,
Turkeys and hens in the yard, turf from the bog,
And to keep the faith in the parish of Parke,
In the one-street village of Turlough, County Mayo.

In 1949 she gave me the run of the tap room
At five years of age
With a dessert spoon to scoop up porter
From the enamel white tray under the hooped barrel to
    savour
The life-giving black draught with the foamy cream
    bubbles.
In 1952 she got red roaring mad with me

For singing 'A Nation Once Again' in the open counter
    leaf
And as she gave me a roasting
Her sunny red face blackened with grief.
'I don't want to hear that nonsense in this house!'
(In 1923 the IRA had put her father up against the wall;
You could still see the bullet holes in the gable.)

At the foot of her grave, down below in the valley,
The French windows of the library door of the landlord's
    house,
Before whose four blue-grey cut limestone steps
Her father's father stood in line
With all the other tenant farmers of Turlough
To doff his cap and pay his rent –
His rent to breathe the air and cultivate a patch
By grace of the lords FitzGerald of Turlough –
The landlord's agent bestowing a liquid smile
Upon the dry, crisp, lined pages of the ledger rent book,
Until one day her grandfather cursed the landlord to his
    face,
The landlord evicted him and her father was born
On the side of the road under hawthorn and sycamore;
The landlord's house today a public museum and the
    glinting library windows
Are silver-cuffed, dreamy attendants in livery at her
    sleeping feet.

Amidst the vintage of her laughter and her porter,
Of her anger and her litanies to the Virgin Mary

I learned to talk with the dead and to love life.
The two yew trees at the gate to the graveyard
She planted with authority fifty years ago:
The two yews sentinel to the daylight moon
Either side of the gate;
Two virginal daughters in bottle-green homespun;
Her identical twins grown to eighteen feet tall;
The only sound the odd footstep of my own.

Paralysed, bed-ridden in her room in a nursing home,
A crenellated Victorian Gothic mansion in a bog,
She commanded me to climb up on a straight-backed
  chair
And, stretching out my hand across the top of the
  wardrobe,
Hunt for a brown paper bag and place it on her
  bedspread
And open it. In a nest of pristine white tissue paper,
  gleaming,
Two dozen silver teaspoons.
'You're not to tell the Judge I gave them to you!'
(The Judge was my father, her brother.)

On the morning she died two heroes of the IRA,
September 16th, 1974,
Separately arriving at the houses of two judges in Belfast,
Shot them both dead in front of their daughters
As they were eating their breakfasts, cornflakes and sugar,
So that old daily Ireland might be a nation once again;
All that pure pedigree, miller's fraulein, racial opining.

I lie down in the grass beside my aunt Sara Mary's grave
In the dying sun for a nap
And gaze out of the oriel windows of time
Down at her far below in the estuary of eternity
Tinkling in a breeze from the south west
And heaving herself starboard into her doom,
The prow of her pride anchored by her prickly humility.

O generous woman to whom no mean man dare tell lies
Or squeal rats' cries,
For you there are only big open changing skies.
She bustles out of the rear base of her headstone
Calling out the password of the Resurrection:
''Ospital! 'Ospital! 'Ospital! 'Ospital! 'Ospital!'

Heatwave

I explored for two miles along the coast
In my bare feet in the shallow waves
Under a cloudless sky, the shore empty
But for a young couple
In their swimwear, a plane
36,000 feet overhead, a tractor
Baling hay in a cliff-top field,
My head emptying,
The waters rising and falling on pebbles and stones,
Bits and pieces of marine biology,
Philosophy, history, images, ideas
Of Fondane, Celan, Rezzori, Char,
Romania, Moldavia, the Bukovina, the Vaucluse,
The Hapsburgs, the Russians, the Muslims, the Jews,
My feet crab-like in sand and water,
Becoming aware again of the couple in front of me
In their swimwear
Because she had jumped up on him and planted
Her legs around his waist and he
Was having difficulty keeping his feet,
But he did, for another ten seconds,
Staggering around like a juggler punch-drunk,
Before she jumped down and dragged him down with her
And I looked away and I knew
That that was the right thing to do, to give them back

The empty shore to do what they had to do,
There was no going back now for either of them,
And I asked if on a golden day on a purple shore
Is there anything else for a human being to do
But copulate, kill, eat, be killed, nurtured, massacred,
Be single-mindedly unwise,
Be uncharacteristically contemplative,
Be buried, be embryonic again, curled up, evacuated
In the gardens of Wexford, in the valleys of Lebanon?

The Seal of Burrishoole

I know I will be killed by my family.
In Ireland, that is our way.

Bury me in the estuary
When the tide has gone out
Uncovering the track;
Under wine-red boughs of mid-winter
And faithful yellow furze;
Where seaweed is all over
And six cows stand apart from one another
Along the spine of the drumlin,
And a sea breeze blows from the west
And in the gap of the estuary
The seal of my death
Poised on a rock as it always has been.

Bury me in my raincoat
With my worry beads in my left hand
And the hem of my raincoat well above
My bare, bare feet.

I know I will be killed by my family.
In Ireland, that is our way.

At the Funeral in Gardiner Street Church of a Ninety-One-Year-Old Priest

Six feet three, he was, I measured him myself,
Oh, about thirty years ago,
For a cardigan my mother wanted to knit him.
Six feet three and a bit, actually, in his boots,
The old-fashioned big black boots with laces and
    eyelets.
He was a priest here in Gardiner Street church
For close on fifty-two years.
He was grand, manly, and when he smiled
You would have sworn he was a general merchant
Or somebody like that; he smiled
As if the world belonged to him and he owned
    everything in it,
And of course, in point of fact, he owned nothing,
Seeing as how he was a Jesuit priest here in Gardiner
    Street.
Worshippers came in their droves to hear him,
Especially on Sunday mornings in Lent.
He'd get that cross about the devil and all to that,
His cheeks used turn scarlet and black with fury
Under his big thatch of white hair
And his voice used make the whole building

Look as if it was about to quake.
You could have heard him down in the docks.
But then when he was doling out Holy Communion
He was angelic, an old dote.
Really, at heart, you know, he was a big baby.
Do you know something else? He loved the sea.
Nothing pleased him more than to chat about the sea.
He'd have been a film star if he hadn't been a priest.
Do you know who he reminded me of? Vincent Price.
The sort of man that if he had to cut up a lady with a
    knife
He'd do it nicely, like, you know what I mean.
He was so kind and caring and thoughtful.
My sister used help him with his Christmas cards.
He'd send out hundreds, she used tell me, hundreds.
She knew because she used lick the envelopes for him.
Oh he was that humble, and dignified and, well, saintly.
I never knew him to have a day's sickness,
Not even a head-cold or a stomach ache.
Ah, he had super genes, you know, super genes
And his marbles were nobody's business
And every week on a Friday night
There was a harem of women outside his confession box.
They queued to tell him their sins.
They'd have done anything for him, anything,
And so would I. We adored him.
I think his confrères were a bit, you know, well, jealous.
But what could they do? They didn't have his genes –
    or his marbles.

Noel Sheridan

What do you do when you read that a comrade has
    died?
Do you groan and sigh, 'God rest his soul'
And continue with what you are doing,
Washing dishes and making phone calls?
Or do you bellow with anger and disbelief
And fling the casserole dish on the floor
And go for a four-mile walk by the sea
Between whose white horses you glimpse him?
NOEL SHERIDAN IS DEAD and
I will be doing nothing else today
Except sitting on the bridge in the village
In my torn wellingtons and frayed gansey
Waiting for someone who is never going to come,
But doing my best to be a faithful retainer
In the Russian play of life starring Noel Sheridan
Who onstage wears a wide-brimmed black hat and the
    largest smile
To be seen west of the Volga and a voice to match,
Nasal-broad to wow the cats in Moscow.

Little Girl Watering on the Sands

Little girl watering on the sands
Twinkles as she grips her hem,
Spreads wide her legs,
Peers down at the splash she has made,
Frowns as she analyses
Quickly drying sands:
Surface texture
Of the enigma of what disappears.

For her the passing of water
Is not a euphemism;
What she has performed is comparable
To what Moses did in the desert;
Yet, water having darted from the rock
Transpires to be seepage:
Her demeanour melancholy
At mortality of divinity.

Kneeling at the Last Wave

to Jarlath Cunnane

Up there on the stony shore of the North West Passage
you might unearth tears in a man's eyes;
you might unearth even a grimace of compassion;
even the undertone of a premonition of affection.

Seafarer, these are my bones
and here is lichen on my skull:
crimson-scabbed, beige-intaglio'd lichen on my skull.
The different shall inherit the earth, if there are any
    different left.

Badgers

to Veronica Bolay

At dawn they came in, flying low,
Fighter bombers, grey with black stripes.
Mother crawled on her hands and knees
Through streams and forests.

The operations manager of the mobile phone company,
Requesting his chauffeur to stop the Mercedes
On the back-road on the south slopes
Of the mountain, uncapped his binoculars
To peer across the sheep-flecked valley
At the whitewashed cottage with the red galvanise roof.
By the gold face of his Rolex wrist-watch
It was 8 a.m. on a summer's morning
And, as before, there was turf smoke faltering
From the squat chimney.
He remembered, as before he had remembered,
The first time he had visited,
How the woman of the house had offered him tea
And she had asked him:
'Would you like herbal tea or green tea?'
And he had laughed with her, a thing
He had never done with a woman before.
Laughed with a woman!
He had answered: 'I'll have normal tea'

And how she had laughed
And how finally he had offered her a half-million euro
And she had said no, no to a half-million euro,
And again he had laughed with her.
To laugh with a woman, at least that was something!
He had said: 'I am sorry to badger you'
And she had said: 'Oh but I like to be badgered by you'
And she had stepped out of her low-heeled shoes
And surged in her bare feet to the grass-fringed edge
Of the flag of the sill-stone
And his polished laced shoes had rippled a reflection
Of his hurried face.
Putting the caps back on his binoculars,
Requesting the chauffeur to drive on,
Leaning on the elbow-rest in the back seat,
Pawing the knees of his pinstripe suit,
He asked himself what a badger looked like.
Unseen to him, under her cottage on the mountain,
She sat on a rock, her toes clawing wet grass.

At dawn they came in, flying low,
Fighter bombers, grey with black stripes.
Mother crawled on her hands and knees
Through streams and forests.

Newsdesk

The bad news is that I buy a newspaper every day. The good news is that I do not read it.

Women of Athens

Down and out in Athens in the dying sun
I learn where to hang out and not to hang out.
I pass much of the day in Cathedral Square
Pacing up and down under the plane trees,
Gazing up at the clock tower, sitting
On a bench next another white-haired vagrant
With a pair of pliers in his hands,
Mooching in and out of the cathedral
Whose crimson-curtained west door is always wide open:
The Cathedral of the Annunciation of the Virgin Mary.
Loitering at the back of the cathedral in Athens
I am appalled by the explicit devotion of the women of
    Athens.
Of all ages and classes they come and go
Singly or in couples or in families.
The more chic the woman –
Is there a woman in Athens who is not chic?
In Athens there are no women in tracksuits –
The more chic the woman, the sleeker, the foxier,
The more devout she is,
The more openly, extravagantly, unashamedly devout
    she is.
She lights her candle and she stands in front of her icon,
Kissing it, thrice making the sign of the cross, from her
    waist bowing.

In hip-clenching blue jeans, low-cut skin-tight black
    blouse,
High-heeled lime-green boots up to her knees,
Long, damp, curly hair running down her breasts,
She surrenders herself with abandon to her icon.
I am appalled, never having witnessed
Such flagrant devotion in my native land;
Ireland, reputedly a religious country,
But which now I realise is not a religious country;
In Ireland nobody surrenders
And churches are but memorials to death.
Here in the Cathedral of Athens at twilight in autumn
How can I be a part of flagrant devotion to the gods?
A voice says: But you are a part of it now
In the wall of your complaining, in the ground of your
    beseeching.
Come down, Paul, from your perch of pride,
Come down off the Areopagus Hill
And like the women of Athens become a free spirit
Before the iconostasis blazing.
Let nobody again ever tell you
That you are not a free man, especially when
Down and out in Athens in the dying sun.

Greek Woman of High Standing

She wears black always, always black,
Black blouses, black skirts
That cling and do not cling
To her limbs in the sun-wind.
Smitten by her
In the porch in Athens,
The caryatid second from the left,
I had not known such mental passion
Transfigured by the physical;
Such feminine intensity
Articulated in intellectual forms.
Her long black hair when she let it down
Flowed down her spine-delta
To converge and diverge in the small of her back.
She stood alone with her arms by her sides,
A caryatid carrying the world on her head.
There was no book she had not read,
Only Proust had been delayed for a rainy day,
That type of rainy day that never really comes to Athens
Except in monsoon-downpours, typhoon-floods.
O Caryatid, did you carry me, too, on your head
In the beginning of time?
And all these handsome, glorious boys standing
Around us suffering from manic depression –
Did you carry each one of them too?

The weight of the weight of the world?
Did you, while walking in the market place,
Soak up the sweat of Socrates on your forehead?
Osmosis? Telepathy?
She said: 'My theme is loyalty
In a world of betrayal.'
I cried to her: 'You must come to bed with me!'
The groin-centred male,
At my feet a sleeping dog of Athens,
The spitting image of my dead father,
That sallow-faced visage.
I meet a caryatid and I think of bed!
She cried: 'That is out of the question!
I have a house to support,
A vision of reality to be installed on the plate of my head!'
Greek woman of high standing,
She is a column of support in a crumbling world-order,
The apotheosis of femininity.

Epistemology

If there is nobody to share the world with,
There is no world.

The Moment of Return

Life and death would never be the same
After that morning in the square outside the cathedral
　　in Athens
On 'No Day' – the anniversary
Of the day the Greeks said 'No' to Mussolini –
And the armed forces were all lined up in platoons in
　　the square,
The Douanier Rousseau panoply, peaked caps with
　　gold plumes,
White gauntlets, white cinctures, red braid, brass buttons,
Epaulettes, stripes, medals, motorbike cops in vulture-
　　postures,
Bandsmen writhing in tubas, policemen in cordons
　　dragging on fags –
Dainty sailors with bayonets on their shoulders,
Tourists, prostitutes, clergy, locals,
Stretch limos decanting government ministers and their
　　wives,
When he chanced to glance up at the steps and he saw
　　standing above him
A young uniformed policewoman in a blue mini-skirt,
Black nylon stockings, black stiletto high-heeled shoes
　　with pointy toecaps.
She was standing sentinel on the south side of the
　　square, near the west door,

On the top step, with her back to him, her small, soft
    hands folded
Under her bottom, clutching gloves, white gloves.
All the staircases of his life, all the treads and raisers
    came back to him,
Those years when after long hauls to Brazil and New
    Zealand and Japan and Australia and Canada,
Finally after all the longing for home he made it back
    home
And he put his bag down on the floor of the kitchen
And she took his hand and led him lazily up the stairs
To her bedroom and gradually pushed him onto the
    foot of her bed,
And began to undress him, and he her, until neither of
    them knew
Which was the sea and which was the skiff as they
    crested the waves,
Sheets and pillows and quilts cascading above them
As they approached the headland, the sacred headland,
Each lost in the roofless temples of the other's hands,
And memory and oblivion were one. The young
    policewoman high on her heels
Shifted from ankle to ankle, tilting on her stilts,
And he knew that no matter how close to death he
    might be,
He would want first and last the moment of return, the
    union of Greece and the soul, of the hereafter with
    the preamble, the blank white cartridge paper of
    incessant surrender.

Walking with Professor Dillon in the Old Agora in Athens

After what seemed like hours in the noonday heat,
    fatigue, perspiration,
Exasperation with one another for no good reason,
Having strayed up and down the old market place in
    Athens,
Pottered, toppled, paced, crawled
To and fro its alleys, olive groves, stone arcades
And clambered up a hill to the Temple of Hephaistos
Where under the frieze Professor Dillon remarked
Of woman-throttling man-beasts:
'Wine did not agree with centaurs – centaurs
Got rambunctious on wine . . .'
We spotted what appeared to be the only bench in the
    Agora,
In the shade of a clump of cypresses, facing east,
The sun high in the western corner of the southern
    quadrant.
Capturing the only bench
We fell to talking about *Reise-Angst*,
That species of anxiety unique to travellers:
Why it is that some of us feel compelled to arrive at
    airports
Or railway stations with an hour or more to spare.

We talked of Estonia, the Irish language, his father
　　Myles Dillon,
Of stamp collecting in the 1950s,
Of Archilochus of Paros, poet of love and war,
Of Yannis Ritsos of Crow Street, Athens, of Desmond
　　O'Grady
Of Paros also, Alexandria and Kinsale, of Michael
　　Hartnett
Of Foley Street, Dublin, of whom, paraphrasing E. M.
　　Forster
On Constantine Cavafy, Professor Dillon remarked:
'He stood at a slight angle to the universe.'
He remarked also on the great age that Socrates lived
　　to
Who walked these self-same paths all those centuries
　　ago,
That man of barefoot reasonableness.
Our conversation was significant for its gradual flow,
Its ease and silences, without tension or attention-
　　seeking.
Suddenly I heard myself exclaim: 'Look, John!'
And he looked and there not five metres from his
　　toecaps
A tortoise had emerged from under a cypress
To commence its navigation across the footpath to the
　　other side.
We watched in silence, face-making in admiration
But also in thanksgiving that we had been blessed
By an order of being outside ourselves,

That we had been ennobled by the company of a
    tortoise
And its lifestyle. Pausing at many intervals,
The tortoise, an empress in procession,
Conferred on each of us original virtue, that first
    permission,
That license to live which we so infrequently obtain.
The tortoise stopped and seemed to utter:
'Dillon, John, Regius Professor of Greek:
You are indeed the magnificent scholar that they say
    you are;
Durcan, Paul, visiting poet: after all these multifarious
    years
You are entitled indeed to call yourself a poet.'
The tortoise trundled into undergrowth and vanished;
With a lightness in our feet, although drained and
    famished,
We retraced our steps across the old Agora of Athens.
The terrors of the day ahead seemed to lose some of
    their ferocity,
Obstacles seemed surmountable, the difficult almost
    desirable.

Par for the Course

While the American and British armies were landing
    on the beaches of Normandy
And de Valera was keeping Churchill, Roosevelt and
    Hitler at bay
And Hyde was counting in Gaelic the raindrops on the
    windowpanes in the Phoenix Park,
Sheila was a twenty-eight-year-old bride blossoming in
    pregnancy,
In her fifth month, her rains drenching all the paddocks
    and boreens of her body,
Anticipating with fearful delight the birth of her first
    child.
Her consultant gynaecologist, Dr Burke-Wykeham of
    Fitzwilliam Square –
Known as 'Wee-Wee' to all the ladies of Dublin
On account of his diminutive size, scarcely five feet tall –
Was reckoned not only one of the best in the business
But also one of Dublin's most eligible bachelors
For his double vents, his large lapels,
His silk handkerchiefs, his bow-ties,
His bouffant silver hair and his annual income,
Estimated at fifty thousand pounds sterling a year.
A room was booked in the Stella Maris nursing home
And when the night came, a windy October night,
At first Dr Burke-Wykeham was nowhere to be found.

The nun in charge tittered to Sheila's husband:
'Wee-Wee is fond of a wee drop, you know.'
Her husband was livid, but he could say nothing
Because Wee-Wee was a power in the land;
As well as having played rugby union for Ireland,
He was on first-name terms with government ministers
Whose wives he knew better than they did themselves;
Of all their lineaments and configurations
He was their accountant and statistician.
In the nick of time Wee-Wee showed up
But such was the trembling of his hands
At the moment of delivery he let slip the forceps
With the result that the face of the newborn infant
Was red as a squashed tomato. The young mother
Expressed her dismay, but Wee-Wee brushed aside her
    fears,
Informing her that it was par for the course, that
He would put the baby's face in ice for a day or two
And all would be right as rain. Mother and son
Left the Stella Maris with the boy sporting
A permanent red eye – a botched delivery –
And this red eye he carried with him for the rest of his
    life.
'It's only a birthmark,' Wee-Wee assured his mother.
The bewildered mother had no choice but to take up
    that refrain,
Which she repeated to all comers for the next
    fifty-eight years:
'It's only a birthmark.'

The MacBride Dynasty

What young mother is not a vengeful goddess
Spitting dynastic as well as motherly pride?
In 1949 in the black Ford Anglia,
Now that I had become a walking, talking little boy,
Mummy drove me out to visit my grand-aunt Maud
   Gonne
In Roebuck House in the countryside near Dublin,
To show off to the servant of the Queen
The latest addition to the extended family.
Although the eighty-year-old Cathleen Ni Houlihan
   had taken to her bed
She was keen as ever to receive admirers,
Especially the children of the family.
Only the previous week the actor MacLiammóir
Had been kneeling at her bedside reciting Yeats to her,
His hand on his heart, clutching a red rose.
Cousin Sean and his wife Kid led the way up the
   stairs,
Sean opening the door and announcing my mother.
Mummy lifted me up in her arms as she approached
   the bed
And Maud leaned forward, sticking out her claws
To embrace me, her lizards of eyes darting about
In the rubble of the ruins of her beautiful face.
Terrified, I recoiled from her embrace

And, fleeing her bedroom, ran down the stairs
Out onto the wrought-iron balcony
Until Sean caught up with me and quieted me
And took me for a walk in the walled orchard.
Mummy was a little but not totally mortified:
She had never liked Maud Gonne because of Maud's
Betrayal of her husband, Mummy's Uncle John,
Major John, most ordinary of men, most
Humorous, courageous of soldiers,
The pride of our family,
Whose memory always brought laughter
To my grandmother Eileen's lips. 'John,'
She used cry, 'John was such a gay man.'
Mummy set great store by loyalty; loyalty
In Mummy's eyes was the cardinal virtue.
Maud Gonne was a disloyal wife
And, therefore, not worthy of Mummy's love.
For dynastic reasons we would tolerate Maud,
But we would always see through her.

Major John MacBride's Early Morning Breakfast

At 3.37 a.m. in the dark
Major John MacBride was cut down by firing squad.
For Mummy life would never be quite life
And there would never be breakfast in bed.

Treasure Island

On his sixth birthday, October 16th, 1950,
His mother took him to see his first film.
If she had promised him only a bus ride
Into the city centre
He would have been frantic with expectation,
But not only did she take him on a bus ride
Into the city centre – the Number 11
Into Nelson's Pillar, just she and he alone
In the front seat together on the upstairs deck –
But on disembarking in O'Connell Street
She took him by the hand and steered him
Up the steps of the Metropole Cinema.
This new, until-now forbidden world of cinema
Was a second extension of his mother's bedroom
(The first extension being the parish chapel):
The red carpets, the gilded mirrors,
The brass stair-rods, the swing-doors within swing-doors
Like veil upon veil of a temple
Proceeding to an inner sanctum, the plush
Tip-up seats, the hush when the lights dimmed,
The girl acolyte strapped to her tray
Of tubs of ice cream and beakers with straws,
Floor-to-ceiling wine-red curtains being parted
To reveal the forbidden silver screen, and he
Seated beside his mother in the public dark,

Safe in the abyss, gazing up
At the soft black rain of her hair,
Her mouth glistening with plum-red lipstick,
Her white pearl necklace, her white pearl ear-rings.
What could be more vista-rich for a six-year-old boy
Than to be seated in cinema darkness at his first film
With his young mother, his first sweetheart?
Larger-than-life pictures on the screen
Filled him with freedom, longing, dread:
When horses appeared on the crest of a hill,
Galloping cross-country to the port of Bristol,
He ducked his head in his seat for fear
Of being trampled to death by their onrushing hooves.
Long John Silver made a grand entrance
As the buccaneer to beat all buccaneers,
Parrot on shoulder,
With a glass of rum and a gleaming eye,
And his unshaven, bristling black chin
And his one leg and his West Country piratical voice
    and
A small boy on his sixth birthday gripped tight his
    mother's hand.
The first film of his life she had chosen
To bring him to was *Treasure Island*
Starring Robert Newton as Long John Silver,
Denis O'Dea as Dr Livesey
And Spike Milligan as Ben Gunn.
In his cinema seat he became Jim Hawkins
Sitting in secret at the bottom of the barrel,
Overhearing things a boy should never overhear.

For the first time he understood
That the price of knowledge is death.
When they emerged out of the film
As out of a book of the Old Testament,
Day had changed into night and it was raining;
All of Dublin was black water and city lights
And his mother queued for a Number 11 bus.
They sailed home aboard the *Hispaniola*
To the coal fire and the brass tongs,
By which they lolled until he fell asleep.
As surely as God created heaven and earth
Thenceforth, aged six years, his life,
In all its people and in all its places,
Would be a *Treasure Island*
A tropic idyll forever under threat,
A geography revealed to him by his mother,
Sweet Sheila MacBride, who had married John Durcan,
One of the black, red-roaring, fighting Durcans of
    Mayo.

Mother's Altar Boy

Although from infancy I was mad to go to Mass
In University Church on St Stephen's Green,
All those vestibules and winding stairs,
All that gilt in darkness, all that white marble in gloom,
The balustraded pulpit half-way up the wall,
The red arched door to the inner sanctum,
Plush red carpets, golden brass rods,
Sunday morning theatre with seats in the front row of
    the balcony,
Always the same play running, always by the same
    playwright,
Always the same exits and entrances, the same costumes,
The candles, the bells, the cruets, the chalices,
The shrine that I worshipped at most fervently
Was not the altar of God
But my mother's dressing table in the sacristy of her
    bedroom.

My mother was a young priestess of the Forties and
    Fifties,
Much given to devotion in front of her mirror,
Vesting and divesting, applying oils and creams,
Ointments and unguents and scents,
Consecrating herself before the divine looking-glass
And I was her altar boy, attending her faithfully.

77

Applying her lipstick and powder-puff with devout
    attention
She sat upright on her stool in clouds
Of corsets, petticoats, stockings, suspenders,
Garters, slips, knickers, brassieres.
There was only one discordant note and that was the
    framed-
In-black wood photograph on the wall of the Pope,
A black-and-white head and shoulders portrait of Pope
    Pius XII
Or 'Pacelli', as in Ireland he was more usually called:
Many a new house was named 'Pacelli'
(Which house do they live in? They live in 'Pacelli').
Eugenio Pacelli – the lean Roman aristocrat
With the implacable facial features of the clerical
    diplomat.

Staring down at my mother in her private oratory
Practising her devotions among womanly things,
Pacelli's countenance was not a reassuring countenance,
Pacelli's stare was a stare of disapproval.
For reasons that I as her acolyte could not fathom
The instruments of her passion
Did not appear to sit well with Pacelli.
Petticoats, corsets, stockings, suspenders,
Garters, slips, knickers, brassieres
Did not appear to find favour with Pacelli.
Although he himself wore long ball-gowns,
Frilly under-clothes and fur jackets,
Her perfumes appeared to offend his nostrils;

Every time I dared to glance up at Pacelli
His nostrils appeared to be in the act of flaring.
But my mother paid no attention to Pacelli.
My mother attended to her personal devotions
As if Pacelli was not there. She whirled around
Smiling down at me, sheathed in her lingerie:
'Well how do I look, my little man?'
Pope Pius XII was not bowled over.

Crime and Punishment

Zig-zag sunlight in May, a young mother
Having spent the morning in St Stephen's Green,
Sitting up against a tree with a claret-red Penguin
    paperback,
Crime and Punishment, Dostoevsky, her favourite author,
Her seven-year old son, her firstborn,
Sailing his dinky boat in the pond among ducks and
    swans,
Before the walk home up Lower Leeson Street,
Elects to nip in to University Church
To get confession, she going first, peremptorily,
Confessing the usual prescribed sin, 'impure thoughts',
Of which she has never had any in her life
As far she knows but she has to confess something,
Penance of three Hail Mary's and an Our Father
And 'a firm purpose of amendment' and an act of
    contrition, her little boy
Stumbling in after her, nervous, but he's nervous
About everything, it's his nature, poor child,
Only for the priest to fling open the confessor's door,
His door, the priest's door, jump out and grab
The handle of the penitent's door, the confessional
    door,
And unleashes out of his trap-door gob a
    spittle-throated roar

At her seven-year old son, castigating him
For not following the proper protocol of Holy
    Confession:
'Confession is a sacrament, you little pup!'
She, thin, shy, fatigued, recuperating from pleurisy,
Asks the priest why he is roaring at her son.
He roars at her: 'How dare you
Speak like that to a priest!' Her son in tears of fright
Gripping her frock, her voice suddenly surfacing:
'Father, how dare you speak to a child like that,
You are not fit to speak to a child,
You should be ashamed of yourself,
You conceited, foul-tempered old ninny! I have a mind
Never to let my child go to confession again! I have a
    mind
To tell my husband who is a judge about you.' The
    priest
Stares down at her, her son stares up at her,
Both of them struck dumb by her leaping anger, by the
    whale
Of her anger, and in the silence
She holds hands with her son and she plunges out of
    the church,
Never again in her life to kow-tow to a priest.

War and Peace

She is forty years old and Dr Burke-Wykeham,
The gynaecologist with the golden fingers,
Has advised that the time has come
To dispense with the double-bed. Has not Pope Pius XII
Proclaimed it an obligation
In cases of married couples who have finished having
    children,
Who have done with procreation?
On an airy early summer's afternoon in 1956
She is lying in her new single bed in her old married state
Feeling ill, not knowing why;
Her eleven-year-old son jumping up and down at the
    foot of her bed
Crying: 'Mummy! Mummy! Get up, get up!
The film of your favourite book is on in the Adelphi!'
But she says that she is not feeling well enough to stand
    in a queue
And everyone is talking about the length of the queues
    for *War and Peace*.
He throws himself down on the end of her bed,
    disconsolate
Not only at not being able to go to the new film
But at the inexplicable spectacle of his mother pallid and
    listless.
He jumps to his feet: 'I know what we'll do,

I'll stand in the queue for both of us. It's only three o'clock.
I'll cycle down now, and stand in the queue
Until the next screening at seven o'clock. You can catch
A bus down for seven o'clock.' She bursts into laughter
At the intensity of his simplicity.
Down the stairs he races three at a time and away on his
    bike.
Like a new courting couple they meet up in the foyer at
    seven,
He brandishing two tickets like a victor with the trophy.
During the three and a half hours of the epic film
Whenever he glances up at her, she is entranced,
And this gives him such pleasure he cannot measure it.
He is drunk with admiration for Natasha,
For her eyelashes and her bosoms, and he knows
That one day in the distant future he will marry Audrey
    Hepburn.
His mother is drunk with admiration for Henry Fonda as
    Pierre.
She is drunkenly smitten. By the end of *War and Peace*
She has married Henry Fonda, her own husband the
    judge having regrettably dropped dead on the golf
    course,
And Pope Pius XII having also died, in Moscow
    mysteriously,
And through the long winter of 1956 to 1957 every cold
    dark evening in Dublin
Henry Fonda, who is also secretly in Moscow,
Comes home in the rain with flowers for her in his
    dripping hands.

Philadelphia, Here I Come

When her husband the judge had their nineteen-year-old
    son
In the Spring of 1964
Committed to St John of God mental hospital
She was not consoled, but she was helpless.
The judge said that the doctor knew best
And what the judge said was law:
'All this calling himself an athlete is an escape;
All this running is malingering;
The doctor says he has schizophrenia
And, therefore, he *has* schizophrenia.'
After he had done six months a release date was set
And to celebrate his release she booked seats
For herself and her son for a new play
At the Gaiety, *Philadelphia, Here I Come.*
Mother and son had a rare night out in the freedom
Of the grand circle of the packed Gaiety Theatre
But neither of them afterwards spoke about it.
Each was fearful the other might criticise and spoil it.
On the bus home they basked in one another's
    satisfaction,
Their cheeks glowing in reticent aftertaste.
The play was about a young Irishman, Gar O'Donnell,
Who was emigrating to Philadelphia
On account of his inexplicable estrangement from his father,

A quandary familiar to the nineteen-year-old boy
Tasting freedom after six months incarceration in a mental
    hospital
In the company of sedated, rebellious priests committed
    by bishops.
He identified, as critics say, with the emigrant,
But although he could see that his mother was enjoying
    the play
He did not understand that she too identified with the
    emigrant,
Only more vigorously than he did.
The playwright, a new name, Brian Friel,
Had two actors, not one, playing Gar O'Donnell,
Gar Public and Gar Private,
And the ex-mental hospital patient's mother Sheila
Immediately saw onstage her own kitchen table:
At one end Sheila Public and at the other end Sheila
    Private,
And on either side facing one another
Husband and son bickering, skulking, carping, scowling.
Sheila Public sat in helpless silence
Enduring the pair of them, interjecting
The odd futile, conciliatory phrase;
Sheila Private sat in manic hilarity
By turns mocking and scolding the pair of them,
The two males in her life whom she loved,
Yet who caused her almost nothing but grief.
Schizophrenia, here I come!
Philadelphia, how are you!
For unlike the emigrant in Brian Friel's play

A forty-nine-year-old mother in Dublin in 1964
Had not a slave-girl's chance in Egypt of emigrating
anywhere.
Ahead of her another forty years in Dublin
Listening to the same old argument, the same old inces-
tuous nightmare.

The Wrong Box

When her son – not for the first time having wound up
In a hostel for homeless boys in London – was
    committed
To a mental hospital, and when from a social worker
    she learned
That he had been incarcerated in the leucotomy ward,
Her husband did not want to know about it – but she
    did;
Alone she took the plane to Heathrow, Easter 1966,
Booked into the Regent's Palace Hotel in Piccadilly,
Succeeded in obtaining a Day Pass for her son,
Met him on a bench in Leicester Square, asked him:
'Would you like to come to a film with me?'
'Which one?' he asked. 'You decide,' she replied.
'*The Wrong Box*,' he said, which was the big hit of the
    day,
Knowing nothing about it except that it starred all
Of his favourite comedians: Tony Hancock, Peter Cook,
Dudley Moore, John Le Mesurier, Peter Sellers.
They got up from the bench under a leafing maple,
In sunlight of reconciliation crossed Leicester Square
To the Odeon where they sat in the empty dark for
    three hours
Watching *The Wrong Box* which, whatever else it was,
    was the wrong film.

Possibly also it was the worst British comedy film ever
   made.
When they came out of *The Wrong Box* the sun had
   gone in,
The wind was chilly, her eyes blurred with tears
As she kissed him goodbye, he running for the Epsom
   train
Back to the mental hospital, she going down into the
   Underground
To take the Piccadilly Line to Heathrow – 'in the
   opposite
Direction to Cockfosters', her husband had warned her –
Her husband always had a great sense of direction –
'The judge has a great sense of orientation' –
To catch the Aer Lingus Viscount flight back to Dublin
And the curt 'How was he – what did you do with
   him?'
'We went to a film' – 'What was it called?' –
'He has got terribly thin, it was called *The Wrong Box*.'

Nineteen Eighty-Four

Mother and son were star-struck by George Orwell.
In 1960 she had obtained a paperback copy of *Nineteen Eighty-Four*
From her spinster sister who had been on a visit to England,
The complete unabridged Penguin Books edition
Which was banned in Ireland and which was not a book
Considered proper for a married woman to be reading,
Much less a judge's wife.
The judge was unaware of it. When she had read it
Her sixteen-year-old son read it. Both were dismayed by it.
The imagined world of Orwell's novel was more real
Than the unimaginable year of 1984
Which was twenty-four years down the road ahead of them.
Orwell's imagined world was as real as yesterday's bad dream.
It smelled of betrayal and winter and sour milk.
It was their least favourite of Orwell's books.
Her favourite Orwell was *The Road to Wigan Pier*
And her son's favourite was *Down and Out in Paris and London*.
The next twenty-four years went by in a bottle of smoke

And 1984 began with the death of Andropov and the
    expulsion of her son
From his marital home in Cork and his refusal to tell
    his mother
His whereabouts. But what she suspected was true –
That he was down and out in Dublin and Cork.
After three months of searching for him,
Worried out of her mind as to whether he was dead or
    alive,
She found him in a shelter for homeless men at Dun
    Laoghaire Pier,
A derelict, Victorian, three-storey house on a terrace
Overlooking the Holyhead ferry. On an April day
They walked on Dun Laoghaire Pier, she out of grief
Upbraiding him for not telling her of his whereabouts.
In a meat-eating wind she gave him a big piece of her
    mind.
'The least you could have done was to have told me
    yourself
That your wife had thrown you headfirst into the
    gutter
Instead of me having to hear about it second hand.
Do you realise that I thought you were dead or dying?
Have you forgotten that for all forty years of your life
I have prayed for you as well as supported you
First against your father and then against everyone else?
You have fallen so many times we have all lost count
But at each fall I did my best to help you
To get you back on your feet, but now you tell me
That this time at the age of forty you cannot get up

And that all you want to do now is to lie down and
    die.
I'm not going to let you lie down and die.
Don't tell me you've completely forgotten George
    Orwell.
It's time now for you to book into a B&B
And I am going to help you to do just that.
Tomorrow morning I'll collect you in the car at 9 a.m.'
The seventy-year-old mother put her gloved hand in
    the bare hand
Of her forty-year-old son and turned back into the
    teeth of the gale
On Dun Laoghaire Pier,
Dodging the spray from the high waves of the sea.
It was a bright, cold day in April, and the clocks were
    striking thirteen.

Daddy and Mummy

What are Daddy and Mummy doing?
Daddy is giving Mummy a golf lesson.

What Mother Loved

She always loved riding horses in the rain,
But what she loved most was playing golf in the sun.

Mother Playing Golf in a Bikini

The summer that Mother started to play golf in a
    bikini
Was the first summer that cracks began to appear in the
    façade
Of family life, fissures in the granite and red brick,
At first indiscernible. Fifty years later
It was remarked by those who are inclined to be wise
    after the event
That her eldest son, namely myself,
Had a fetish about women and the clothes that women
    wear
Or do not wear; that I was hung up
On what was revealed or not revealed
By strips of clothing that covered or did not cover –
And I cannot deny that this is true, and was true,
Not only of me but of my father also.
I am a male for whom there is a mystique
About women and the first woman I ever knew was
    my mother
And the second woman I ever knew was my mother's
    mother.
I think that for my father and I
When my mother started to play golf in a bikini
She was asking of us to become members of the
    Church of England,

Of which her mother in the 1890s had been a member
And that was something neither of us was going to
    find easy to do
On the shores of Killala Bay in the County of Mayo.

Golfing with Mother for Great Britain and Ireland

Golfing with Mother for Great Britain and Ireland
On a nine-hole seaside links in Killala Bay
In the summer of 1957, high on survival,
Hungary and Suez behind us,
The fortieth anniversary of 1916,
Rented houses littered with back issues of *Time*,
I asked Mother if we were golfing also for America.
She put a finger to her lips, the little finger of her right
    hand,
And she let slip that smile of hers that seemed to say:
'Oh you are a naughty boy, but you are no daw!'
I knew then that on the altar of my righteous idealism
I could install Eisenhower alongside de Valera and
    Macmillan.
On the seventh hole, the world simplified itself:
The correct way to speak, the model family, 1916.
I was a championship boy on the winning side
Golfing with Mother for Great Britain and Ireland –
    and America.

The Gallows Tree

Your father was an old-fashioned man,
A man of reams of words or no words at all.
It was always either a feast or a famine.
You couldn't shut him up or
You couldn't get a word out of him.
The day he proposed to me in 1942
I thought he'd never come to the point,
But that was what made him interesting.
He was always dawdling, your father,
While he was talking, always digressing,
Turning down side-roads of a conversation,
Stopping in a gateway he had not noticed before.
We'd been driving around Mayo all day
Revisiting the old haunts and he was talking
Ten to the dozen about Michael Davitt
And the Land League, how that blackthorn bush
On the side of the road was where Michael Davitt
Was born, and that Michael Davitt
More than Daniel O'Connell or Charles Stewart Parnell
Was the man who really set Ireland free
And finally we stopped in Castlebar
And we walked up to the Mall
And it was a lovely evening, but a bit chilly
Because the sun was going down and he started
Into George Robert FitzGerald again,

George Robert FitzGerald of Turlough
And what an extraordinary young buck he was,
Chaining his father to a bear and being
A devotee of the Hell Fire Club in Dublin
And winning every duel he fought
And how he was sentenced to hang
And how right here on the Mall in Castlebar
On the gallows tree the rope broke
And how George Robert FitzGerald
Lost his notorious temper for the last time
And upbraided the hangman for not knowing his job
And how George Robert told the hangman
He'd teach him a lesson
And George Robert in a towering rage
Hanged himself on the gallows tree in front of the mob
And your father turned around and said to me:
'Sheila, there's something I want to ask you,
I've been wanting to ask you for a long time,
Will you marry me?' And I said, 'Yes'
And he said, 'O Sheila, my own'
And he started to cry.
Your father was an old-fashioned man.

Clohra

Happiness? (*Pause*) It was summer of 1939,
The summer that Clohra, my eldest sister –
She was ten years older than me,
A solicitor with her own car,
With her own office in Westport,
The first woman solicitor in Mayo,
A woman way ahead of her time –
Invited me to accompany her
On a driving holiday around Ulster:
Donegal and Derry and Antrim.
'There's going to be a war, honey,' she laughed.
'Soon we won't be able to go anywhere.'
I was starting in a new job in Dublin
In the Land Registry on September the 1st.
She drove all along the north coast
From Donegal town to Belfast city,
I mean the actual coast roads,
Every seaside village and small port,
Killybegs, Portnablagh, Dunfanaghy,
Portnoo, Bruckless, Marble Head, Culdaff,
Portrush, Portballantrae, Cushendall.
We met our MacBride relations in the Glens
And we heard how only a generation ago
We had been Protestants –
How we laughed at that.

What I remember now is the sunny weather
And Clohra at the wheel, always laughing,
At the wheel of the Morris Minor;
Her huge bosoms hanging down
Over the rim of the steering-wheel;
'The last pumpkins in Versailles,' she yelled.
She didn't plan the route,
She didn't book ahead.
In the evenings she simply decided to stop
Wherever we happened to find ourselves.
She'd spot some small, old-world hotel,
The sort of place that doesn't exist any more.
We had our rackets and clubs in the boot
And usually after tea we'd play
A game of tennis or a game of golf.
She'd pick up whatever young fellows
Happened to be about – there were loads,
Bank clerks, locums, strays.
In the ten days there was not one unpleasantness.
She was always in such good form,
Always thinking of funny things to say,
Kind things, interesting things.
Whenever we passed a car
Coming from the opposite direction,
Clohra put her hand on my knee and cried out:
'Happiness, Sheila, that's happiness.'
In bed at night, we shared the bed,
We read novels to each other,
Tolstoy, Turgenev, Dostoevsky.
In Belfast on our last day

She insisted on buying me a fur coat –
Clohra who could not afford such a thing.
A fur coat not
For herself but for me!
I tried to stop her
But once she got an idea into her head
There was no stopping her.
Even when fifty years later
She got Alzheimer's
There was no stopping her.
There was never
Any stopping Clohra.
On our last night in Belfast
We walked the avenue up to Stormont.
Next day I got the train to Dublin
And she drove back to Westport,
My gorgeous, darling, eldest sister.
Then on the 1st of September I started work
And that night we heard the war had started.

Cleena

Cleena, Clohra's twin,
At the age of sixty-seven
Has pulled up stumps
And come to live in Dublin,
Having lived all her life
In County Mayo,
In the small town of Westport.
At the age of sixty-seven!
I feel like crying.
When I call around to her room,
A rented room in Leeson Park,
She is down on her knees
With a pair of scissors
And mountains of newspapers
And magazines –
The *Irish Independent*
And *The Divine Word* –
On the floor all around her.
I cannot help shrieking:
'What are you doing?'
She replies
With that infuriating mixture
Of hers
Of meekness and obstinacy:
'I'm cutting out things.'

'Why?' I shriek. 'Why?'
Offended, she replies:
'For future reference.'
If she sees anything
To do with 1916
She cuts it out
'For future reference.'

I drive back around the corner
To my three-storey home
In Dartmouth Square
With its nine spacious rooms
And I sit down and fume.
She says she cannot stay with me
Because she'd be a nuisance,
But we both know her real reason:
My husband. She's afraid
Of my husband, the judge.
He is six feet tall.
She is four feet eleven.
She weighs seven stone.
She is white as a sheet.
She has high blood pressure.
She doesn't feed herself.
She's got a stutter
Like a torrent pouring upwards.
She goes to two or three masses a day.
She goes to one or two films a day.
She phones me from a coin box and asks:
'Would you like to see *Valley of the Dolls*?

Would you like to see *Of Human Bondage*?'
She likes, she says, Julie Christie's face.
We both like Julie Christie's face.
All the rest of the time
In her room that reeks
Of newspapers,
Of mouse urine,
But also of Dettol
And where it's always dark
She spends among clippings,
Sifting, sorting.

O my dearest sister
It is 1972,
But for you
It will always be 1916
In the month of May
When you were eleven
And Uncle John
At 3.37 a.m.
Was led out
In the dark
Into the stonebreaker's yard
In Kilmainham jail
And executed
By firing squad.
By a volley!
We could hear it
In Westport.
We could hear it

For the rest of our lives.
The constabulary took away
Our father,
Put him in prison
In England.
Our dear old boy.

O Cleena, Cleena
Whom our father loved
More than any of us,
What are you doing
At the age of sixty-seven
In a rented room in Dublin
With brown paper bags
Of newspaper clippings?
Each clipping most
Carefully, neatly folded
And dated in your slanted
Handwriting in blue ink.
What will become
Of all these brown paper bags
When you are gone
And there is no more 1916?
Your brown paper bags of newspaper clippings,
What is to become of them?
I am fifty-seven and you are sixty-seven,
Little sister. Am I dreaming?
I see you crossing the quay
At O'Connell Street Bridge
In front of a double-decker bus.

You try to avoid it, but you cannot.
You clutch hold of its one outsize all-hoovering
    windscreen wiper
Clinging on to it, thinking the driver will see you
And he does, but what does he do?
He ignores you, little sister, he ignores you,
Red blood trickling out of the corner of your mouth,
O Cleena, Cleena, WAKE UP!

First Place in Ireland

Only on bridge nights
Did she break free,
Mrs John Durcan
With her partners three,
Other lawyers'
And doctors' wives:
Mrs Tom Eustace, Mrs Jerry O'Mahony,
Mrs Andy O'Keeffe.
At ten they broke for tea
And cake, and the frenzy
Of hoots and screams
Resounded in the back gardens
Of Dartmouth Square.
Forty years of age
In matrimony's cage,
She who at twenty-one
Got first place in Ireland
In her final year law exam
To become an outstanding
Young solicitor,
But who five years later
Was compelled by law
On marriage to resign
Her solicitor's job
To marry a barrister,

Give birth to his children,
Two sons and a daughter,
Rear them, mind them
While he was away
On the Western Circuit,
Five days and nights
Alone in Dublin
In a Victorian square
With three infant children,
Marooned,
Housekeeping, skivvying,
Never again to have her own money,
Never again to know
The pleasure of a day's work,
Of being a good professional,
Of being independent,
Of enjoying the company
Of her peers,
The camaraderie of her colleagues,
To watch her husband
When he became a judge
Become a recluse,
Not a dog in the manger
But a shadow in the bedroom,
Who every afternoon
Lay down with the curtains drawn,
His Ireland-in-the-Fifties face
A brolly of pessimism,
Spokes protruding,
To cook his meals

And wash his underclothes
For forty-five years.
Instead of researching the land laws
In relation to tenure and ownership
And altering society by applying
Her mind to these questions,
She applied her mind to the question
Of whether or not she could afford
To buy a washing machine
And later a pressure cooker,
A fridge, a dishwasher.
In 1944 she was the owner
Of a washboard and mangle,
But by 1954 she owned
A washing machine
And by 1957 a dishwasher,
She who had got
First place in Ireland.
Instead of being famous
For her brilliance as a lawyer
She became famous
For making cakes and ice cream;
Her ice cream with chocolate sauce,
Her orange sponge cake and her meringues
Made her famous in the family;
Her barm brack studded
With brassy thrupenny bits;
The Sunday roast lamb,
Although she could do it with her eyes shut,
Took hours to prepare and put

On the table for half-past one,
When her husband returned
From the golf course, the Sunday
Morning four-ball
To which the muezzin called all
Middle-class Irish males in the 1950s.
At night she wandered off
Alone to her bed
With a mug of Bournville hot chocolate
And a saucer of biscuits,
Lincoln Creams, the new
Biscuit of the era.
'She had that many brains, your mother,
You could have dipped your fingers in them.'
Small surprise
That at the end of her days
In her eighties,
The little scraped barrel of her,
The thin-lipped scream of her,
The spittle-stoppered mouth of her,
She was spilling
Over with rage,
She who on a summer's day
In 1937 in the law
Got first place in Ireland.

St Stephen's Green after Heavy Rain

Sitting alone on a park bench with my handbag
I think I have something – not a lot
But something – in common with that blackbird
Poking about in the wet grass under my feet.

Under the trees I too am a bird alone,
A middle-aged mother, a contradiction in terms.
My children all grown up and gone, my husband
Gone to play golf with his four-ball.

Only yesterday I was a young mother
Circled round by lots of other young mothers;
Certain that we would live forever
With our children who would be always young.

That young man on the next bench with his bicycle;
He seems not to have a single pocket.
His sleeveless shirt, his short pants,
Where does he keep his money and keys?

O my bold young man with not a care in the world
It is right that you should be carefree,
Yet I cannot help but worry as I watch you
Cross your legs and fold your arms

That you might come to grief on your bike,
That your life also is a life in the balance;
Intestines and blood cling-filmed by a membrane;
A heart's artery sagging on a saddle.

A middle-aged mother does not live for ever
But nor does a young man with a bicycle,
His face in profile. If only every morning
Was a morning after heavy rain.

Max

All her life Mummy had been dependent on Daddy,
But when he got Parkinson's he became dependent on her
And she took to her role reversal like an old goat to new
    grass.
Commandeering his wardrobe became her priority:
She got rid of the grey suits and the drab casuals
And dressed him up in yellow plus fours and green
    jumpers
And a selection of tam-o'-shanters, pixies, caps.
Daddy protested, but he adored it
And she reverted to addressing him by her pet name for him
From the days of their courtship in the early 1940s, Max,
And you could see that he much preferred being Max to
    being John.
One of my last memories of Mummy and Daddy
Is of the pair of them in their seventies
On a late spring afternoon in Palmerston Park:
She leaning up against a pine with a bouquet of white
    roses in one hand,
Holding the hem of her skirt in her other hand
And Daddy in his oldie-buggy in yellow plus fours and
    green jumper
Gazing up with glee at her.
At last, if only for a late spring afternoon,
Sheila and Max were back in their element.

Doctor Zhivago

Fifteen minutes before her husband's death,
Seated in her lilac overcoat at his bedside
As he lay dying in a public ward
Of a centre-city hospital,
In his blue-and-white pinstripe pyjamas
She had ironed the day before yesterday,
Denuded of the privacy
Which more than any other one thing
He had sought all of his days,
Suddenly, as he began to navigate the death-throes,
A boatman in a torrent,
His oars flummoxed,
She took his hand, clutching it tight in hers
And, her fingers knitted in his, she wept.
It was the first time they had held hands
Since that night in 1966
On her fiftieth birthday
He had taken her to see *Doctor Zhivago*:
Oh John, for the love of God
Let me carry your cross.

The Deposition

At the crucifixion of her husband
In the public ward of a centre-city hospital,
After he had been taken down from the Cross,
Wheeled out to the mortuary,
Contemplating the appalling deposition of him,
His matted, stained, dried-up skeleton,
The battered woman in her lilac overcoat,
Mrs Sheila Durcan, formerly Mrs John Durcan,
Stood by his forehead, her right hand exposed,
Her left hand clutching at her groin,
Her eyes up on the ceiling – fluorescent lighting, is it? –
Voting for women, that was something –
Wanting only to be beside him in the next life
And for the pair of them not to be cold,
Maybe under that Foxford rug we bought in 1948
With the bunch of purple heather we picked near
    Boniconlon.
It's so cold in this mortuary, isn't it? So wretchedly cold.

Daughters of the Civil War

How could we have known, we who were the
    daughters of the Civil War,
That before we were young women we would be old
    women?
That we would not have time to climb the mountain
Before the cold fog of marriage leg-ironed each one of
    us.
How could we have known, girls on the virgin
    seashore,
That by the end of the Thirties our lives would be over
And that although some of us, such as I in my silk
    girdle,
Would survive into our eighty-eighth year
For most of us life would be over
By 1942 and the Battle of Stalingrad,
The year I got engaged to be married?
How could we have known that as well as Collins and
    Childers
There were other murdered men who had shaped our
    lives
And how a woman is no more impregnable than a
    seashore
And for no shallow reason picks the wrong man?
There was Niall and Nevin and yet I chose John
And if the reel could be rewound back to its source

There again would be Niall and Nevin, but again I'd
    choose John.
A woman has to choose the man who is wrong
Over and over again
As if she were fast asleep,
Otherwise how would she know she was the same
    woman?
How would she know the names of the men who'd
    been slain
In her childhood in the Civil War when she had been
    fast asleep?

Little Old Lady

Mummy shrank as she grew older.
After Daddy died, she became so small
She began to look like a little girl
And, after a period of grief,
To disport like a little girl – the little girl
In the photograph album of 1927
Making hay in Mayo, raking, tossing it,
In the summer before her twelfth birthday.
At seventy-three she beat her way out of the lethargy
Of old age and she began to hop about
Not only the apartment but the city streets,
Beginning conversations with strangers at bus stops
And hanging out in the new space-age shopping centres.
From a sports shop catalogue she purchased
A steel-and-rope trapeze, which she installed
In a niche over the kitchen door.
'It's compact,' she confided one lunchtime.
'It folds up and folds down like a dream.'
After I'd washed up and dried the dishes
She demonstrated it and teasingly
Tried to persuade me to buy one for myself.
On the morning of her eightieth birthday,
When I'd brought her a gift of a bucket of begonia,
To my chagrin she showed only
A perfunctory interest in my begonia,

Which I had gone to some trouble to purchase.
Instead she stood on the seat of her trapeze
Mocking me as she swung to and fro,
Her little white tennis skirt fluttering
Above her matchstick knees. She cackled:
'Now what do you think of your little old lady?
Do you think she is surplus to requirements?
Well, don't think I'm fishing for compliments.'

The Jolly Stone-Carver

In her eighties
Gussy Loneliness –
That jolly stone-carver –
Chipped away at Mummy
Until one day when I visited her
And she opened the door
There were two little old women
Huddling there instead of one.
She laughed, as she always laughed
At my discomfiture,
And having piped, 'Are you not coming in?'
She explained: 'The jolly stone-carver
Has detached me from myself,
Let me introduce you.
She can entertain you
While I boil you an egg.'
The other lady
Was a little old girl
With the legs of a ten-year old
And the face of a crone;
She sat on the sofa in a swoon
While I went into spasms of stammering.
'Oh for heaven's sake,' she cried
'Give over that stuttering,
You are well able to utter.'
In the kitchenette we sat down
At the egg-timer on the card table,

Topping our eggs.
Mummy mused: 'I wonder
What Bertie is thinking
When he's topping his egg?'
Between her skinned digits
She crushed the eggshell,
Roaring into the sitting room:
'I say, I wonder
What Bertie is thinking
When he's topping his egg?'
'How would I know
What Bertie is thinking
When he's topping his egg?'
'I don't know
How you would know.'
'Then give over.'
'Oh leave me alone.'
'The trouble with you
Is that you are too old
For Bertie, but you will not
Accept it.'
'I despise Bertie.'
'You hero-worship Bertie.'
'No, I do not.'
'Yes, you do.'
'It is you who
Are Bertie-bitten.'
'How dare you!'
'How dare you!'
'You are a howl.'
'So are you.'

September 11, 2001

Eyes and ears are bad witnesses to men whose souls are always savage.

Heraclitus

Swaggering the sandy-banks among hundreds of sheep
I stumble upon a sheep on the shelf of a sand-hill,
Asleep on its side, only as I step
Close up to it, it does not make
A move to move its glossy black face:
Just like Mummy that afternoon
Two weeks before her eighty-sixth birthday.

Creeping back up the Haw's Lane at twilight
I come upon a second sheep shelved
Under a low dry-stone wall under a sycamore,
Snug as a suckling in its mother's lap.
Nor does it make a move to move;
Just like Mummy that afternoon
Two weeks ago before her eighty-sixth birthday.

I opened the door of her allotted room,
No 318 in the Winston Nursing Home;
Spotless, void as a new prison cell
Except for her prone body face to the wall
Strewn on the narrow stainless-steel bed;
Just like those two sheep today
As I swaggered the shores of the western ocean.

The first sheep on the shelf of the sand-hill
Was in perfect nick, except that it had no eyes;
She had irrevocably travelled on to the next world.
The second sheep under the wall had eyes
That were open, but were not seeing things;
She also was en route to the next world.
Mummy made no move to move.

I stand in the doorway like a sheep-killer.
Her underclothes are scattered on the floor.
She makes no move to move.
Is she alive or dead?
A male custodian opens and closes the door
Just like out of a gangster movie;
Is he a nurse or a hit man?

On a bright Friday morning in the month of August
They came to her apartment and took Mummy away,
Permitting her to bring with her only
A small suitcase and three John Hinde postcards
Of her native town, Westport in County Mayo.
What is your name? What is your date of birth?
Get a move on and take off your clothes.

Oh Mummy, poor sheep – 1930s star –
See what you get for marrying a man
And raising a family and surrendering
Every possibility under the sun and the rain
For the sake of your husband and your children!
They take you away on a bright blue Friday morning
Just two weeks before your eighty-sixth birthday.

Here you lie crumpled at the end of the story
Alone in a state-of-the-art prison cell
With a small suitcase and three John Hinde postcards!
Eighty-five years and fifty weeks equals
A small suitcase and three John Hinde postcards!
Oh Mummy, poor sheep, are you dead or alive?
Just two weeks before your eighty-sixth birthday.

A week to the day after her eighty-sixth birthday,
Tuesday, September 11, 2001,
Just after lunch in the Winston Nursing Home,
Squatting in the day room in front of the 42″ TV,
Mummy along with her fellow inmates keeps
One eye on a plane crashing into a skyscraper.
Smiling, she whispers: 'The same old story.'

Her smile turns into a scowl.
'I get tired of the same old story, don't you?'
'I – I – I –,' I begin,
But my stammer gets the better of me.
'What on earth are you trying to mumble?'
Mummy screams at me through her deafness,
Through her scrunched eyes glaring at me.

The 42″ TV flows on, with the sound turned down.
A skyscraper – is it the same one? –
Is on fire and then a second skyscraper beside it
Falls down, erupting in smoke-spew like lava.
We stare at it, for there is nothing else to do.
Mummy hisses: 'I hate this place.
I will never ever come to a place like this again.'

On my arm she limps to the lift,
I shepherd her back upstairs to her room,
Her pristine, gleaming, death-row cell.
Perched on her bed-edge she points at me:
'You are a sight for sore eyes.
Come here and let me look at you.
Let me have a good look at you.'

She clutches me by the neck and peers
Into my eyes like a pathologist
With a microscope at the scene of the crime.
She cries: 'What will I do?
What am I going to do?'
Except to hold her hand and stammer
There is nothing I can say to her, nothing true.

Who was a young mother on her back,
Sick with laughter, on the sunny shore,
Is strewn on her bed
Like a model in a fashion shoot.
Her sheep's eyes staring at me,
Imploring all that sheep's eyes can implore:
Why hast thou forsaken me?

On autopilot I stammer the words
Of Rhymes and Psalms – the only words
That mean anything to Mummy,
For whom men's words are measly
Or beastly or better not said at all:
Baa, baa, black sheep, have you any wool?
I will lift up mine eyes unto the hills whence cometh my help.

Golden Mothers Driving West

The inevitable call came from the Alzheimer's nursing
    home.
Mummy had been sitting there in an armchair for two
    years
In a top-storey room with two other aged ladies,
Deborah O'Donoghue and Maureen Timoney.
Three Irish orang-utans, silent, stationary.
The call was to say that between 3 and 5 a.m.
The three of them had gone missing from the room.
At first it was thought that all three had slipped
Out the window, ajar in the hot, humid night.
But, no, there were no torsos in the flowerbed.
It transpired that a car had also gone missing.
Was it thinkable they had commandeered a car?
At five in the afternoon the police called
To say that a Polish youth in a car wash in Kinnegad
Had washed and hot-waxed a car for three ladies,
All of whom were wearing golden dressing gowns –
Standard issue golden dressing gowns
Worn by all the inmates of the Alzheimer's nursing
    home.
Why he remembered them was that he was struck
By the fact that all three ladies were laughing
For the ten minutes it took him to wash the car.
'I am surprised,' he stated, 'by laughter.'

At 9 p.m. the car was sighted in Tarmonbarry
On the Roscommon side of the River Shannon,
Parked at the jetty of the Emerald Star marina.
At 9.30 p.m. a female German child was taken
To the police station at Longford by her stepfather.
The eleven-year-old had earlier told her stepfather
In the cabin of their hired six-berth river cruiser
That she had seen three ladies jump from the bridge.
Her stepfather had assumed his daughter imagined it
As she was, he told police, 'a day-dreamer born'.
The girl repeated her story to the police:
How three small, thin, aged ladies with white hair
Had, all at once, together, jumped from the bridge,
Their dressing gowns flying behind them in the breeze.
What colours were the dressing gowns? she was asked.
'They are wearing gold,' she replied.
Wreathed on the weir downstream from the bridge
Police sub-aqua divers retrieved the three bodies,
One of whom, of course, was my own emaciated
    mother,
Whose fingerprints were later found on the wheel of
    the car.
She had been driving west, west to Westport,
Westport on the west coast of Ireland
In the County of Mayo,
Where she had grown up with her mother and sisters
In the War of Independence and the Civil War,
Driving west to Streamstown three miles outside
    Westport,
Where on afternoons in September in 1920,

Ignoring the roadblocks and the assassinations,
They used walk down Sunnyside by the sea's edge,
The curlews and the oystercatchers,
The upturned black currachs drying out on the stones,
And picnic on the machair grass above the seaweed,
Under the chestnut trees turning autumn gold
And the fuchsia bleeding like troupes of crimson-tutu'd
    ballerinas in the black hedgerows.
Standing over my mother's carcass in the morgue,
A sheep's skull on a slab,
A girl in her birth-gown blown across the sand,
I shut my eyes:
Thank you, O golden mother,
For giving me a life,
A spear of rain.
After a long life searching for a little boy who lives
    down the lane
You never found him, but you never gave up;
In your afterlife nightie
You are pirouetting expectantly for the last time.

Mummy Dead

to John Richardson, her neighbour

On a trolley in the mortuary,
Before the embalmers get to work on her,
She is a housefly on the table-top
After having been swatted by a newspaper.
Her thinned snout agape, her eye-sockets scooped out,
Her high forehead soaking in sweat no more.
Her skull a sea shell
Rinsed by the oceans and the tides
Of eighty-eight years of weeping and twinkling.

My Mother's Secret

Like all women of her generation
My mother had a secret,
Which was that as a young woman
In Paris in the 1930s
She had played the oboe,
But that when she came home
On the eve of war and got married
She put away her oboe
And never played it again.
Only *she* had the key
To the locked drawer
In the dressing table
In the marital bedroom.
Did she in her last years
In her show-stopping loneliness,
Distracted, disorientated,
At night in the mausoleum of her flat
In the red-brick apartment block,
Unlock the drawer,
Take out the silver oboe
From its satin couch
And put it to her lips
And, kiss of kisses,
Shock of shocks,
Horn of horn,

Blow on it?
Did Mrs Balbirnie in the next flat
Hear sounds in the night?
After she died
And her grown-up children
Had divided up
Her personal effects,
I trekked to the edge of the cliff
Above her childhood home
On the west coast of Europe
And holding out my two hands
I presented her silver oboe
As a parent presenting
A newborn baby
To the priest at the altar
Before letting go of it
To watch it plummet
Down into the opening-up beaks of the rocks.